Online Marketing Genius

Your Unofficial Guide to Building a Business with Social Media and Serving the Multitude

Brimo Morales

Online Marketing Genius © 2020 by Brimo Morales. All Rights Reserved.

All rights reserved. No part of this book may be reproduced or transmitted in any form or by any means, electronic or mechanical, including photocopying, recording, or by an information storage and retrieval system – except by a reviewer who may quote brief passages in a review to printed in a magazine, newspaper, blog, or website – without permission in writing from the Author. For information please contact the Author by email at brimo@brimagraphics.com.

Published in the United States of America.

First edition, 2020

Published by Brimagraphics LLC

ISBN 979-8-63001-809-0

To my beautiful wife Annette, for always believing in me, my parents for being there when I needed them the most, and all my mentors along the way. None of this would've been possible without all of you!

INTRODUCTION	**V**
CHAPTER 1 SPEAK THE LANGUAGE	**1**
CHAPTER 2 TYPES OF CONTENT	**17**
CHAPTER 3 MAKING YOUR MEDIA LOOK SEXY	**28**
CHAPTER 4 HOW TO COME UP WITH ENDLESS CONTENT IDEAS	**44**
CHAPTER 5 CONNECTING WITH YOUR AUDIENCE	**55**
CHAPTER 6 PSYCH 101	**63**
CHAPTER 8 THE FUNNEL	**79**
CHAPTER 9 WHAT MAKES CONTENT GO VIRAL?	**84**
CHAPTER 10 HASHTAGS AND KEYWORDS	**92**
CHAPTER 11 MAXIMIZE YOUR CONTENT QUICKLY	**95**
CHAPTER 12 PUTTING IT ALL TOGETHER	**102**
NOW YOU'VE GOT TO BELIEVE	**106**
RESOURCES	**111**

Introduction

When I signed up for Myspace my freshman year of high school, (somewhere around 2004/2005), I had no idea what social media was. The concept didn't really ring much of a bell and I didn't get the point of it. Why was I suddenly updating my profile with graphics (as if I were some MIT coding genius) and songs that played automatically? Why was everyone posting bulletins answering questions and making announcements?

I had been in a few chatrooms in the early days of AOL, I loved AOL Instant Messenger, so talking to people online wasn't a new concept, but social media in itself was this crazy new thing that everyone needed to be a part of for some reason. I had no idea that years later I would see the impact it could have on businesses and how people purchased everyday items; how much power it could give us, or how it could spread a message all the way across the globe.

When I first discovered the power of social media marketing I was living in Southern California, working a full time job with an hour (at least) commute each way. There were countless days I'd come home exhausted, neck and back aching, grumbling barely a hello to my wife, before I collapsed in front of the TV for an hour before getting ready for bed.

I wasn't happy with where I was in life, let alone my financial state or the fact that my time was wrapped up in someone else's vision. I had no idea there were ways to make money with social media. I thought the only ones making money were the YouTube stars that raked in millions of views with their videos, but I was mistaken.

While on one of my days off from work I was scrolling through my newsfeed when I stumbled across a video of a guy that said he made over six figures online. Like any rational human being, I thought he was full of shit. Curiosity got the best of me though, and I ended up looking into it more. I realized he actually wasn't full of shit, but he knew what he was talking about and that there were other ways to making money online aside from shooting videos for YouTube and hoping to get paid for ad views. The method I learned was through marketing online.

This started the two-year journey I went on learning as much as I could about marketing on social media. From growing a following, to finding products I wanted to market, to creating my own and also starting my own marketing podcast, Brimo Live Journey To 6 Figures. I've tested multiple methods, got pulled down various rabbit holes, and even met a ton of new friends along the way.

    This book is a compilation of all the things that have worked for me on this marketing journey, and what I hope will help you in your endeavor. There is no one size fits all method, so if someone tells you there is, they are in fact…full of shit. There's a million ways to make a million dollars, and the same goes with online marketing and building a business or brand on social media. Instead of trying to put together a "sure fire method" to reaching more people and making more money, I'm going to show you tactics to try out so you find the best way that works for you. In my opinion if you follow what's in this book you'll stand out in the noisy crowd of social media, but know that there's no such thing as a sure thing. We are all scientists conducting experiments and figuring out what works for us. Just because something worked for me doesn't mean it's going to work for you, or that it will work in a short amount of time. This takes work, experimentation and a lot of determination to make things happen.

If you ask anyone that's "made it", they'll tell you that it didn't happen overnight. It took them trying different things and taking massive action. While other people talk a lot about how they're going to do something someday, these people actually made someday today and worked hard in order to get those results. Success is not for the faint of heart but, lucky for you, success leaves clues that you and I can follow.

The fact that you picked up this book shows me that you're willing to take action. Good for you, that's step one to making an impact in life and in your business. My mentor told me that imperfect action will beat perfect inaction every time. If we want to be successful we've got to take the actions towards whatever it is we're trying to accomplish. Writing this book for you was me taking that action, that lead me to my goal of becoming a published author. If you don't already have goals for your business or brand I highly recommend you start making some. Then as you read this book you'll be able to see what methods you'd like to try in order to reach those goals. This book is solely focused on using social media to grow your following and to reach more people, which will help you generate more business.

Social media is a whole new way of life. It seems that everyone and their grandma is on these days, and it doesn't look like it's going to slow down anytime soon. Whether you're an entrepreneur, an agency, or a big company, social media is where you need to start spending a lot of your time and energy. You've got to meet your customers where they are.

They log on to read the latest news, catch up with their friends or brag about what their baby did this morning, and it's all out there for the world to see. It's how our community has evolved, and those in business that choose to stay off of these platforms will be left in the dust. Sorry to be so blunt but it's the truth.

So if you as a business entity (or solo venture), have a product or service that you need to share; where do you find the majority of the world? They're not watching TV commercials, or listening to radio ads…they're tweeting, snapping and updating their statuses on social media.

Now it's true that when Lauren from down the street logs onto her Facebook account, the last thing on her mind is what kind of leggings she's going to buy from that good looking fitness influencer, BUT, selling on social media <u>PROPERLY</u>, has some astounding results. Millions of dollars have been made from selling on social media. So now's the time to get in on that!

Before you dive in head first into this modern day miracle though, heed this warning. If you just start blowing up newsfeeds with ads promoting your latest gadget to people that could care less, and all you do is push sales, you will be written off as sleazy, your ad accounts will be banned and you'll be lucky if you can get anyone to pay the slightest bit of attention to your posts.

This book isn't about pushing products, it's going to show you how to create content that people not only like, they'll engage with and eventually, once they trust you, want to buy whatever it is that you're selling. Whether you want to be a social media influencer, or just want to get your product to the right people, this book is for you. It doesn't matter if you have a brick and mortar business, an Etsy shop that could really use some love, or you would just like to build a nice following to help as many people as possible, I'm going to show you easy to implement strategies that can help you win big.

Over the last two years I've studied as a digital marketer, coursing over various different social media platforms and what kinds of content do well on each. I'm going to show you how to get raving fans, do everything you can to make your content go viral, and stand out in the busy world of social media. Now I can't guarantee your results, but I will give you all of my best knowledge that has worked for myself and my mentors, and what you do with that knowledge is your business.

Anyone can learn how to do this, but only those that will take massive action, will reap the rewards. Now's a good chance to ask yourself if you're the type of person that will take action, or if you're the type of person that will just horde as much knowledge as possible but will never do anything with it. Those that have done well on social media are those that take the advice and do something with it.

This book is not some magic formula that will magically get you a million followers in a day. It's also not a shortcut to making millions of dollars on social media either. This is a book of tactics that will stand up for years to come no matter what new social media sites come out. If you follow these tips, stay consistent, and do your due diligence to test out new material and study your data, you will see results.

If all of this sounds good, then keep reading. My desire is to help you crush your goals, so let's do the dang thing!

Chapter 1 Speak The Language

When you go to a foreign country as an American and the native language isn't English, you may have a little bit of trouble navigating around. You're lucky to find a handful of people that can speak some broken English and who may be nice enough to point you in the right direction, but if you want to have an enjoyable trip, and relate to the locals, then the best thing you can do is learn some of the language. The same is true for social media.

At sixteen I found myself in the outskirts of Monterrey Mexico. There in the mountains people lived in houses made up of an array of items like leftover fence wood, sheet metal and tarps. They all had dirt floors, not many had electricity or even indoor plumbing. I honestly don't think you've truly lived until you have to use the restroom in what appears to be someone's backyard, with a toilet encompassed by more scrap wood and a shower door entrance. Being of Mexican American descent I knew a little bit of Spanish, but I was nowhere near fluent. Because I was with my church and a missions' trip organization, we were able to have translators to assist us as we prayed for people and put on short services. The people there were very receptive and were always grateful for the time we spent together. And now I have some great memories of exploring a country I had never been to and the wonderful people I met. Had I known no Spanish, and not had translators I don't think I would've had as great of an experience as I did. There would've been so many things lost in translation because I wouldn't have always understood what the people were telling me.

If you've never used social media before, or you've never used social media to extend your brand and sell your products before, you may feel like you yourself are lost in translation. There's so many different platforms and apps today that it can be super overwhelming and hard to navigate. So in this chapter we're going to start learning a few of the different languages of some of the most popular social media platforms. This is the first step in becoming a presence on social media. You have to be able to get on!

Luckily all social media sites have similar aspects to them, even similar purposes. A lot of them help keep you updated in your loved ones' lives, stay up to date with the latest trends, the biggest news stories, and all in all were put there to connect people together. One of our biggest desires as a human being is to connect with others.

Thanks to the internet, all the True Crime Junkies of the world have a place to congregate away from the judgement of the rest of society who just don't understand their love of true crime. Same with the Keto people. They can get into Ketosis with other Keto-heads and not have to worry about people harping on their butter chicken diet. See, there's something in it for everyone! Including you Mr. or Ms. Business person. You have a group of people out there somewhere that are just dying to be your number one fan and buy all of your products and services.

In order to find your people, you have to learn how to speak the native tongue of the platform that you plan to have a presence on. Honestly the more platforms you can learn will only serve you better in the long run, but when you're first starting out, just stick to one or two until you get the hang of it. You could appoint someone in your company (or your children) to learn the various platforms and inform you on how they work and what posts are going viral.

Going viral means that in a short amount of time a post is getting thousands of views, likes and shares. It's getting a lot of exposure and a lot of people know about it. Going viral is usually a good thing because of how many people can come across it. We'll talk more about going viral in a later chapter but I wanted to make sure you at least understood what that meant.

Jump in with two feet and get down to the basics of the platform. How many characters are you allowed per post? Can you post pictures and videos? Do hashtags work well on this platform? What are the age demographics of users? What is their ad policy and how do you post ads? These are the types of questions you need to ask as you're learning how to use the different social media platforms because it's all very important. Not everything that goes viral on Facebook is going to work on Twitter. You can't post videos as long on Instagram as you can on YouTube.

These are all things you need to know about as you start building your following. My suggestion is just to create an account on your chosen medium and start researching. Look for the biggest influencer (person with a lot of followers) in your field and figure out why they're doing so well. Study their posts, what kind of images are they using? How many words are in their post? What types of hashtags do they use? Are they making any money?

You can look up about how much they're making by going to socialblade.com. This is a great tool to tell if an influencer is legit, or just has a bunch of fake followers thanks to some bot they paid to follow people. (Yes it's a thing and no you shouldn't do it too). Automation is great for some things but building a fake following is not going to help you. In fact, you might just get your account banned and lose everything. People like authentic, so let's stick to that and find some big guns with massive followings that are legit.

The more you study, the more you'll start seeing patterns of the type of content they're creating and how much their followers are engaging. Once you've got an idea you can start modeling the types of content they put out in your own posts. Now notice I did NOT say copy. Copying is immoral and should never be done because there could be lawful implications for your actions, and nobody likes a copycat. Study what they do, model it, but do NOT copy!

You're more than capable of creating your own content, I mean come on you purchased this book so you're already on the right track to making it happen. All you need now is a little guidance and I'm going to help get you there one step at a time. The first step is to pick a platform and start playing around with it. Easier said than done, but if you want to win this is how you do it. You take massive action.

On the next few pages I'm going to breakdown a few rules for some of the platforms. That way you'll have a better idea on how you can use each one correctly and not look like Grandma sending the angel chain messages we have all come to hate. That's not how Facebook works Grandma! Let me show you how it works.

FACEBOOK:

- 2.3 Billion Active Users
- 63,206 Character Limit Per Post
- Pictures & Video Capabilities
- 1.75 GB and 45 Minutes Limit On Video
- Reasonably Priced Ads
- Hashtag Capabilities

Facebook definitely has a lot going for it. As one of the hottest social media platforms out there right now, it's not uncommon for people to have one if they're over the age of 18. It's basically a free for all, with over 2 billion users on it, you'll be able to find an audience that wants to follow you. This is one reasons I love Facebook. Not to mention their ad platform is incredible.

This is where I post the brunt of my ads because I know they'll perform well, I know they'll be reasonably priced, and I know how to choose which audiences I want my ads to reach. They have an incredible tracking system so you can re-target people that have seen certain ads and have even gone to your website. It's also one of the most user friendly ad platforms out there. It takes a minute to maneuver around, but once you get the hang of it, you'll find it's incredibly easy to use. It can even post ads to Instagram as well.

INSTAGRAM:

- 1 Billion Active Users
- 2,200 Character Limit Per Post
- Image Based Platform
- 60 Second Video Limit
- 30 Hashtag Limit
- 15 Second Stories

Instagram is my second favorite social media platform to use. Like Facebook there's a huge user base and its primarily image driven. As a visual person myself, I really like this. Who doesn't want to look at pretty pictures and captivating short videos? When you understand how to use this to your advantage you'll be able to create a following of raving fans. The music artist Rhianna was able to sell out of shoes in just two hours by making a post on Instagram. What could you do with that kind of power?

You can also utilize hashtags to your advantage here as well. In case you were born before 1980 and the # sign is primarily called a pound sign, I'll give you the run-down of the hashtag. Hashtags have been repurposed as a way to tag a post to a certain category so when people search using that hashtag your post will come up. It originated on Twitter a few years back, now a lot of other platforms are utilizing it as well. Instagram is a great place for it, and you potentially get more viewers by using them.

You also have the ability to share posts directly to Facebook. In case you didn't realize it, Instagram is owned by Facebook so both platforms integrate really well together. You can post something on Instagram and automatically share it to your personal or business Facebook page. It's really convenient because you want to be able to reach as many people as possible so posting to more than one platform at a time will save you time and help more eyeballs find your work. Instagram has also taken a cue from Snapchat and added a stories feature.

Instagram stories are up to 15 seconds of video or a still image, and when you sync up your Facebook page, it'll automatically show there as well. It's a fun way to create content with your daily life and people really enjoy watching them. It's basically a mini reality show.

YOUTUBE:

- 1.3 Billion Users
- 2nd Most Popular Search Engine
- 5 Billion Videos Are Watched Everyday
- Average Mobile Watch Sessions Last Over 40 Minutes

If you've ever even considered getting on YouTube, now's definitely the time! There's so many different users and channels, and a lot of the younger demographics out there actually prefer watching things online, rather than on the television. That's pretty crazy!

Social media is basically the new Hollywood, with a lot more freedom and the ability to reach people all over the world. This is the place to be! You can literally create a channel or video on any topic your mind can come across and potentially have millions of people watching it. That's mind boggling!

Not to mention people use it as a search engine, second only to Google, who owns YouTube. I know when I can't figure something out, YouTube is where I go to see a "How to" video on whatever I need figured out. I even watched one once when the guy at AutoZone couldn't figure out how to change the battery in my Kia Soul. I YouTubed it and we got it all squared away.

If you know how to do something, chances are someone else wants to know how to too. Allow yourself to become an authority and teach, create your own show, or talk about an experience that could help others. YouTube can make things happen. It is extremely competitive, but if you utilize the strategies in this book, you'll have a better chance of reaching more people.

Similar to Instagram, you can tag your YouTube videos with keywords so it's easier for people to find them in search. This will also allow your videos to pop up in the "similar videos" category when they watch a video that's closely related to yours. This helps you get more views!

SNAPCHAT:

- 300 Million Users
- 10 Second Videos or Pictures
- The Original Stories Platform
- 70% of Users Under Age 34

When Snapchat first came out, the idea was that you could send pictures to your friends that only lasted 10 seconds. So if you wanted to be funny and not want the evidence to stick around, you would use Snapchat. That was until, people realized you could screenshot the images, whoops.

Either way Snapchat has evolved with a wide array of features like being able to locate friends in the area, and even sending money. It isn't as user friendly to run ads on this platform but people still have success on it so it's beneficial to learn. Find someone that's doing really well on this platform and see why. DJ Khalid is a good option, he's blown up on Snapchat and they love him for it.

A word of caution though, the people at Snapchat have stated that they're not as influencer friendly as other platforms. So if you're goal is to create a massive following and get paid for it, Snapchat may not be the platform for you.

PINTEREST:

- 3rd Highest Search Engine
- A Digital Vision Board
- 250 Million Users
- 75% Of Users Are Women

Pinterest has kind of flown under the radar compared to the other big guns out there. Little do they know, but you can be incredibly profitable if you tap into this ad platform and really understand what works well on Pinterest. So really take the time so see who's doing well on there and what types of posts are showing up at the top, those are doing well.

With Pinterest it's important to have appealing images in your post. Because it's a virtual vision board, all of the posts look as if they've been clipped out of a magazine and posted there for your enjoyment. You can search any topic you want from your wedding, to your dream vacation, to your dog's birthday party. Some people find themselves accidentally spending hours just pinning away. So if this is your first time you've been warned. We all know how easy it is to be sucked into social media.

TWITTER:

- 321 Million Users
- 280 Character Limit
- Started The Hashtag Revolution
- Images and Video Posts
- Re-posting Other Users' Statuses

Twitter took the world by storm when it came out in 2006. It's 140-character limit was a force to be reckoned with and celebrities started jumping on to start communicating with their fans. That's still true today with it's over 300 million users. Before Twitter everyone just called the # either the numbers sign or the pound symbol. Now we all know that it's really a hashtag, and Twitter is full of them.

They even have a trending hashtag feed that you can look through to see what people are talking about. That's a great place to start if you've never been on this platform before. It's a great place to stay updated with what's happening in the world. You can even re-tweet a post that you like so it shows up on your profile. Everyone loves to be re-tweeted it makes you feel special.

LINKED IN:

- Professionals Networking Site
- Business Oriented
- Video and Images Work
- 1900 Character Limit
- 467 Million Users

LinkedIn isn't just about finding your next job. It's turned into a social media platform that can stand up with the rest of the big names in this game. Big timers in digital marketing have realized this and started building up a following on here to add to their social portfolio.

Get on here and do some research to see what's working. You're able to post videos and images, along with links to blogs and other websites. It's a great way for you to share your message with people that might never find you elsewhere. They also have an ad platform so you can get more eyeballs on your stuff. The more platforms you're familiar with and comfortable with, the more people you can reach and build up that following.

This was just a little glimpse into the possibilities of what all of the platforms can do and to help you learn more about each one so you could decide which one would be a good fit for you. Your homework now is to actually log on to each platform and play around a little bit. That's what will tell you if this platform could work for you or not.

Once you've determined which platforms you're going to utilize, knowing how to create captivating content is your next step. So in the next chapter I'm going to talk about different types of content that you can utilize for all of these platforms. The best thing you can do with them is test out what will work for your audience, so play around with all of the different types of content if you can.

Chapter 2 Types of Content

It's not enough to just know about the platforms themselves, you've got to know what content is and what you can actually post on these social sites as well. You can't post videos on Twitter like you can on YouTube. But by this point, I hope you've at least started studying the various platforms so you have an understanding of what you *can* post. In this chapter we're going to talk about different types of content, so that when you're ready to start posting you already have some ideas going forward.

When you think of the word media, what's the first thing you picture? Maybe newspaper articles, news segments, billboards, magazine articles, videos, pictures, it's all media and it's all around us every day. Especially on social media sites themselves. There's a reason the word media is there, because it captures people's attention. Media can easily be swapped out with the word content. I'm not talking about the emotion that's synonymous to the word happy, I'm talking about content, what you post on social media.

Pictures and videos are the types of posts you're going to see the most and probably going to produce the most of. The posts that include either a video or a photo tend to perform better than those without. In the following chapters I'll even be giving you strategies in making your pictures and videos look better, and stand out above others. But those aren't the only types of posts that will do well on every single platform.

If you don't like being in front of the camera, don't fret, there are more options out there for you that don't include putting your face out there for the world to see. The first is blogging. Blogging is incredibly valuable for those that enjoy writing and those that enjoy reading content. Are you the type of person that reads every single Facebook post no matter the length? Then chances are you'll really enjoy writing those types of posts as well.

You can create a blog around any subject that you wish. Just like we talked about in previous chapters about connecting with your audience and coming up with content ideas, you can niche down within your blog and attract a following that's into whatever you write about.

Take Mr. Money Mustache for example. He created an incredibly successful blog, all about investing with little startup capital. He eventually was able to retire early and hang out with his wife and kids whenever he wanted to. He documented his journey and started giving insights to other people that wanted to invest and retire early. He's definitely exploded and helped a lot of people become educated about investing, that may never have been able to before. Mr. Money Mustache made it easier for the average working class person to invest and live their best life. If you haven't heard the Tim Ferris Show podcast episode with Mr. Money Mustache, I highly recommend checking it out.

So what can you blog about? There's got to be something you're extremely passionate about that you can teach others. Brainstorm some ideas and then get to writing. Medium.com is an incredible blog website so you don't to have to start your blog from scratch. And you can star without building an entire website. When you do build a website you can even embed your Medium blog into it. Technology is really cool. So get out there and start telling the world what you can offer them.

If writing really isn't your thing, but you love to talk, then podcasting could be exactly where you need to be. I looooove podcasting! In case you didn't know, I am the host of the podcast, Brimo Live Journey to 6 Figures (you can check it out by going to brimomorales.com) and I have gotten some great results with being consistent and posting episodes weekly, sometimes even daily. More exposure, means more eyeballs falling on your content. So if I haven't driven home this idea yet, then publish every day! I don't care how you're doing it, publish every single day, even when you don't feel like it, even when you don't think you have anything to talk about, just do it…more on that later, for now back to podcasting.

Podcasts are cool because you can listen to them pretty much anywhere. Driving, in the shower, cooking, cleaning, wherever you need a distraction, or want some entertainment but still need to be productive. Every smart phone nowadays has a podcast app of some sort. So there's no reason for you not to be on everyone's phone. The easiest way to get a podcast going and published on all of those apps is by going to anchor.fm. This website is so freaking awesome! It's completely free, super easy to use and you get your podcast on all the major platforms out there. So get started now!

You don't need fancy equipment in order to record your podcast. When Russel Brunson (founder and CEO of ClickFunnels) started, he would literally just record on the voice memo app of his phone in his car. I think he still records a lot of his episodes in his car, except now he hands them off to a sound engineer to make sure they sound good. So if Russel can do it without any fancy microphones, so can you! Done is better than perfect, so get your imperfect podcast out there for the world to hear!

When you want to start getting fancy, you can learn how to use a site called canva.com. Canva is responsible for most of those really pretty Pinterest posts everyone re-pins. They make it easy for you to freshen up your content no matter what it is your creating. They have a free and a paid version of their site, I recommend sticking with free because you actually get quite a lot of features with it. Have you ever thought of writing a book? If you are consistent with posting content, you could easily take that and put it together into your own book. Canva can even help you with the book cover. There's also a really awesome site called designrr.io (link in the resources section) that can take your blog posts and turn them into an ebook for you!

Take this book for example. This is a compilation of all of the knowledge I've accumulated about content creation and digital marketing, so that you're able to take my knowledge and run with it. I wrote this book the old fashioned way though, I literally typed out every single word your eyeballs are reading this very moment. You can create an eBook in way less the amount of time by repurposing your old content.

If you have a blog post that has done ridiculously well and you want to use it again somehow, then you can take that blog, throw it into Canva, create a book cover, and voila! You've just created your own eBook. These are useful as lead magnets inside of your funnel or bonuses inside of your amazing irresistible offer! (If you have no idea what a sales funnel or irresistible offer are, I'll explain more later). Are the wheels spinning in your head yet? Are the lightbulbs going off? If not, they should because this stuff is crazy exciting! You can repurpose your content and create assets that you can use for future offers!

Digital assets are huge! Think of them as products you can give away when someone signs up for your email list, or things you can put together to form a package/irresistible offer that will add a ton of value to someone, or just one off products that you can sell in general. They can do a lot for you and your business if you're willing to take the time to create them. If you're publishing everyday like I said before then you can easily create these assets once you've published for a while.

You can also position yourself as an expert in your space by publishing a book. Just like I've done with this book here, you can self-publish with Amazon's Kindle publishing system. By this point you've probably built up a decent sized following of raving fans that will be incredibly excited to know that you've got a book out that could help them even more! Doing content creation right is going to help you get more exposure, create raving fans, and finally allow yourself to get paid for all of these amazing skills you've developed in your lifetime. It's just up to you to actually get the ball rolling and get started with something. You can't build momentum if you never start posting. So it's up to you to get up and start making it happen.

There's also a ton of power in doing LIVE videos. Like Facebook Live, or Instagram Live. Periscope made it all popular, but now other platforms have jumped on the bandwagon and realized how great they really are. It's fun to be able to interact with people live, and beneficial to get their feedback in real time. It can be scary at first, if you've never done a live video before, but once you get the hang of it you'll see how amazing of a tool it is to produce content and to connect with your audience. This is how I do my podcasts. I shoot a live video from Facebook, download it, take out the audio and then upload that to Anchor.fm. It's easy, it's simple and I've got lots of content out there now.

This is huge in the gamer community thanks to Twitch. So if you're into playing video games and want to connect with other gamers out there, you should jump on Twitch and start broadcasting while you play or just talk about your favorite games. I've seen people have massive success with this platform and there's no reason you can't too.

To do a good live video, check out the next chapter for tips on video, but here are a few other things to keep in mind. Start talking about your topic as soon as you go live. You can do a quick intro and say something like "Hey, Brimo here, and today I'm talking about (topic)." The majority of the people who watch your live video will be watching the replay, so if you ramble on about things that aren't relevant, then you'll most likely not have a good retention of people live, or watching the replay.

Also beforehand, take a few minutes to interact with other people's content. Facebook especially, rewards you for interacting with people, liking their stuff, commenting, and sharing. If all you do is produce content but never interact, your stuff won't be seen as much in other people's newsfeeds, and we definitely don't want that. So take the time to interact with people, they'll appreciate it and want to reciprocate. Also rehearse a few times, and write down what your main points are so that you don't forget them. Being good at going live takes practice, so don't be afraid to rehearse it before you actually go live. You won't be stammering forever, eventually you'll get really good at it. We all didn't come out of the womb walking, it was a process but now you're probably really good at walking. Same idea from practicing those go lives.

Feel free to interact with your audience as you're live, that's the fun part. People love hearing you addressing their questions and giving them shout-outs. It makes them feel good and they'll be more likely to watch your live videos in the future. This is a great way to have that two-way conversation with your audience. Again, embrace the feedback that they're giving you, it's only going to help you with your content in the future, and building that relationship is crucial if you want to be successful on social media. Social media is a two-way conversation, not just you talking. We like relationships remember?

There's also the vlog! Vlog stands for video blog, in essence you're showing people your life and work. Vlogging has become extremely popular thanks to reality TV. Everyone wants to know how everyone else is living their life, so if you want people to get to know you really well, vlogging is a great way to go. It's personable because it's video, people can see and hear your voice. You're showing them the more authentic version of yourself because it's you living your life. Document your life and work, make it interesting and entertaining. You're basically creating your own reality TV show and people will love seeing all the fun things you're doing.

If you want to start slow and work your way up, then pictures are the easiest way to create content. Whether you use a nice landscape type picture with a quote over it, or if you use pictures of yourself and write a story about it, or you can make a video with a stagnant picture and have audio playing over it as well. Pictures are easy and capture people's attention. Who doesn't like reading an uplifting message when they scroll through their feed? If you don't know where to start use pictures. But ultimately start with whatever you're comfortable doing and have fun with it!

Now you have an idea about what types of content to post. In the next chapter we're going to talk about making those videos and pictures you use look sexy! So if you're ready to stand out on social media instead of sinking into the background, let's get to the next chapter!

Chapter 3 Making Your Media Look Sexy

For years, companies have used the billboards you see all around town as ways of advertising. I'm sure there are some memorable billboards in your town that you can remember. Recently here in San Antonio there was a billboard of a man in a blue and black checkered suit that said #MyWifeHatesThisSuit. It was popular and was even written about in a local news segment. It was eye catching, it was intriguing. Who was this guy? Why was he putting up billboards to piss off his wife? It created a little bit of hype.

Have you seen any billboards that have done that? I'm not saying go out there and buy yourself a billboard ad, but there's some things that can be learned from this example. Your media needs to be eye catching. People are constantly scrolling through their newsfeeds on a daily basis. You've got to get them to stop scrolling and pay attention to the things you're posting. You can do that by making your media look sexy. That's what this chapter is all about, and it doesn't have to be super complicated either.

Throw out the idea that you need some super fancy, pricy, camera in order to get great images and video. I've taken plenty of great media with my cell phone. In fact, lately as I've been building my business I've only used my phone. (You can check out my posts on my Instagram @Brimomorales). So don't allow yourself to make excuses about not being able to create great content because you can!

One of the biggest secrets when it comes to making good looking pictures and videos is to have great lighting. And you don't have to be a professional that knows how to measure light. If you can face a window while you take a picture or shoot a video you're ahead of the game!

So in this chapter I'm going to break down how to improve your photos and videos easily, so that your content will stand out and catch your audience's attention. Some of this came from my mentor Chris Stapleton and some of this came from my years of doing photography and video and seeing what worked for me. Let's start with taking pictures.

Picture Tips:

1. Clean your lens

2. Face the light source

3. Make sure the subject is in focus

4. Take more than one picture

5. Study magazines and online photos

6. Move closer to subject to eliminate extra space

7. Lightly edit your photos on an image editor

1. Cleaning Your Lens

No matter what camera you're using, even your phone, it's important to make sure that the lens is clean and clear. If not the image may appear blurry or as if there was a haze around the subject even though there wasn't. No, Casper the friendly ghost is not coming out in your pictures, your lens is just dirty.

Take a microfiber, or other soft cloth, and get a nice clean going so that your images look as good as they possibly can. Good photography and video starts with a clean lens. I know it's super simple, but it's also super simple to forget, so make sure your lens is clean before you start snapping those amazing photos!

2. Face The Lighting Source

Have you ever taken a photo standing, with your back to a window and seen it come out really dark and unflattering? That's because you weren't facing the light source. Light is what makes pictures and video look good so it's important that you know the most basic rule about light. Always face the light source.

In this case it was a window. So when you are taking your own pictures or having someone take them for you, find the light source and face it. I don't recommend staring at the sun and blinding yourself, but I do recommend having enough light on your face so that your picture looks really good.

Play around with your camera/phone and start taking selfies while you are facing a light source. You'll begin to see how much better your pictures can actually look if there's enough light on you. If you find that you are getting too washed out (looking more like a messenger from God) then take a few steps back and take another picture to see if that helps. If you're outside and can't escape the brightness, try standing under a tree or another source of a little bit of shade to help with that. Experimenting is the best way for you to get better pictures and video, so now's the time to start playing around with it.

3. Make Sure the Subject Is in Focus

Let's face it, no one likes looking at a blurry photograph. What could've been a really nice image turns out to be something that looks like it came out of Game of Thrones once Drogon torched King's Landing. You can do better!

If you are mostly going to be taking pictures of yourself, I highly recommend getting a decent selfie stick so that you can stabilize and not have your hand shaking too much. It's very easy for your arm to start getting tired and shake. Having a selfie stick gives you a little bit more arm, and allows you to hold it closer to your midsection (where your center of gravity lies), and allows you to have less chance of blurry pictures.

If you're able to, tripods are also a great tool to add to your tool kit because if you're not even touching them, then there's no way for you to move and make your pictures blurry. You can even set a timer on your phone or camera to take the picture within 10 seconds to allow you to set it and then pose.

Believe me it's completely possible to take amazing pictures by yourself. So don't feel like you won't be able to if you don't have an assistant. It just takes a little practice to see what techniques work the best for you. Of course if you have a friend handy to help you, then use them! You can communicate how you want your picture to look like and your newly found photographer can help you make it happen. I used to ask my wife to take pictures of me all the time.

4. Take More Than One Picture

If you really want to get the perfect picture, then you've got to take more than one picture. Anything can happen to easily screw it up, so by taking more than one picture you've got back-ups just in case. The more pictures you take the better chances you have of finding at least one that you really like.

If you've ever gone to a professional photographer, or seen a shoot on TV, you'll notice that the photographer takes a ton of pictures, not just one. The magazine cover came from a series of pictures and they narrowed it down to the best choice; so too will you be able to choose the best take from your photoshoots.

The best part is, if you've got a bunch of good pictures, you can use some of the other takes for other posts in the future. I really like having an arsenal of pictures on hand for any new post I'm about to make on my social media. That takes away more work later from having to take new pictures every time I want to post something.

5. Study Nice Images in Magazines and Online for Inspiration

You've seen really nice photos before. Just walk through the grocery store and check out the magazines or surf the web for a few minutes and you'll come across professional photographs that catch your eye. What is it about them that makes them nice? The obvious reason is because a professional took them, but why do you like the pictures?

Look at how well lit the subject is, check out how they are framed up in the photo. Is the person or object centered? Or off to one side of the other a little? What kind of facial expression does the person have? Do you notice anything in the background? Does this image make you feel a particular type of emotion? Figure out why that is.

Those are just a few things to think about as you're studying other people's work. You can take an image you really like from online and then try to recreate it yourself. By this point you should've already started studying some other influencers and big shots in your space. What kind of pictures are they putting online? Find one you like and recreate it.

6. Move Closer to Subject to Eliminate Extra Space

As you're studying other images online, I'm sure you've noticed one big thing about all of them. The subject (person or object in the photo) is very large in comparison to the size of the photo itself and there doesn't seem to be any wasted space. If you have no idea what I'm talking about, pick up a popular magazine with a celebrity on its cover. You'll see that the celebrity is taking up pretty much the entire cover. You barely see anything in the background. That's done on purpose.

The subject is the focus of the cover. They were meant to be seen, for your eyes to catch their face. It's like when you're out and about and you make eye contact with someone. It's the same principle. You make a connection with other faces and it makes you want to pick up the magazine and look at it.

This is what you want to do with your images. Make them so captivating that people want to look at them. They want to stop scrolling through their newsfeed and see what it is you have to say about your incredible image. So let them! Get rid of all the negative space around your photo that doesn't matter, in order for others to connect with them.

7. Lightly Edit Your Photos On an Image Editor

If you want to make your pictures look like every other Joe Schmoe on Instagram, then go ahead and use all of the preset filters they already have. We're not here to look like everybody else! We're here to stand out and make a statement! So why not edit our photos differently also?

Now before you freak out and say, "Oh my God! I don't know Photoshop!!" You don't have to. You can edit them right on Instagram, or in any other free photo editing app on your phone. The point isn't to edit it so much that it looks nothing like the original, the point is to make your pictures pop just a little bit. And that's really easy.

All editing apps have things like, brightness, contrast, saturation, and temperature. You can utilize these tools to edit your photos just a touch. Start by adjusting the brightness just a bit, if you find your photo a tad too dark this will help lighten it up. But be warned, when using brightness, if you turn it up too much you'll end up making your photo look fuzzy. Those little dots you see are what we call "noise" and it doesn't look very flattering when noise is all over your image. This is why lighting is so important to all of your images.

Once you've got the brightness where you like it, maybe turn up the contrast a little bit. Contrast makes the shadows harsher and makes you stand out more. If you overdo this one you might find yourself looking like something from a comic book. Play with the settings, you still want to look like a real person, not an illustration.

After you've got your brightness and contrast set up, then you can play with the saturation and the temperature. Both of these settings have to do with the color you see on your pictures. The less saturation you have, the more your picture will start to become black and white. Black and white photos are okay every once in a while, but I wouldn't utilize them all the time because they're not as bright as color photos are.

If you start turning the saturation up, you'll actually see more color added to your photo. Too much and you'll end up looking like an oompa loompa from Willy Wonka. Just saying. Don't use too much saturation, a small amount goes a long way.

Temperature is similar to saturation but focuses more on the red and blue spectrum of colors. By turning the temperature down, you may see your image start to look a little cooler, or blue tinted, while going the opposite direction you'll see your image getting hot, or becoming more red. This is really personal preference, so play around with it and see what you like. You'll also start to notice which images are getting more engagement. You can start editing more of them with those particular settings as you go along. Most of the time less is more when it comes to editing but you'll start to notice what looks good and what doesn't the more you do it.

All of these tips work just as well for video as they do for pictures. So take what you learn from the images and start utilizing them when you start shooting video. The only other things you'll need to pay attention to is your audio, how the video is shot, and then some basic video editing.

What I mean by "how the video is shot", I'm mostly talking about when you're using your phone. It irks me very much when I see videos with black lines on the left and right sides of the frame, because someone doesn't understand the format for which the video is being utilized. This happens when the video is being shot with the phone held vertically.

Vertical   **Horizontal**

When you're shooting video on your phone most of the time, you will want to turn your phone horizontally as you're filming. This way the format that you shoot in, won't have those black bars on the sides anymore. If you look at your television you'll see that it looks like your phone being held sideways, that might help you remember that when filming, you want your phone to be sideways as well.

There are of course exceptions to this rule. Depending on when you're reading this book and what social media platforms there are out there, this might not be as big of a deal. For Snapchat and Instagram stories, their format is perfect for shooting your videos vertically. Then you won't have to worry about black bars, you'll actually be utilizing the platform correctly. So in some cases yes you'll want to keep your phone vertical, but in most, you'll want to shoot horizontally.

When it comes to audio the rule of thumb is, shoot your video in a quiet location. If you are going to be speaking in the video, we don't want to hear cars driving passed you, wind blowing loudly, or super loud air conditioners. Be mindful of where you are recording because if your ears can hear it, chances are the microphone in your phone is picking up the noise as well. Shoot somewhere with little to no background noise so your voice sounds clear and every word is understood. You can use a lapel mic or a directional mic like a shotgun mic, to help with audio, just make sure you record a test version to see what the audio sounds like before shooting the real thing.

The last note is about video editing. I'm not going to teach you how to video edit in this book. It would take too long and two-dimensional teaching doesn't translate well when talking about video editing so I will just give you some quick advice for it. If you are new to video editing, find a relatively cheap or free software. For Windows computers you can use something like Camtasia or Windows Movie Maker. For Apple computers you can start with iMovie or Screenflow.

There's a ton of free video tutorials on these software programs on YouTube so that's a great place to start learning. If you have no interest in learning how to video edit, then outsource and find relatively inexpensive labor on a place like fiverr.com. You can get what you need very inexpensively and all you had to do was shoot the video.

I hope you read through this chapter carefully, because now you'll have a basic understanding of how to make your content look really good and stand out in the marketplace. Your job now is to go out and start creating, from here we'll talk about how to come up with ideas for the content you create without having to stress over it.

Chapter 4 How to Come Up with Endless Content Ideas

A lot of the big gurus of social media will tell you that you need to create content every single day…but they don't always tell you how to actually come up with ideas for that content. I've found that what makes it easy for you to come up with a ton of ideas for content is to learn more so you can teach others.

As we've discussed before, the point of content creation is to get your audience to know, like and trust you. It helps to sound like a real person, not a crazy sales robot that has no feelings and pushes people to buy all day. So where do you come up with ideas for content? It can definitely be overwhelming, but the good news is, you're probably just overthinking it.

We want to get people to know us right? So let's just start there. Pretend that you're going on a date with a really attractive person. What kinds of things do you ask each other on the date? What you do, what you like, where you like to hang out, all the fun stuff! Your audience wants to know about you too!

There's a reason that you're doing what you're doing. Was it because you love skiing so much that you wanted to teach others how to as well? Or because you were done being an employee and wanted to start a laptop gig that would allow you to travel? Either way, something made you decide that this was a good idea. People want to know about that, they want to hear your story!

They want to find those similarities in your life that they can relate to. One of our basic needs as a human is to be in community. So by telling your story, you'll build your tribe very easily. Start with your origin story. If you're unsure about how to tell a good story, I'll show you a basic framework you can use in order to make this easier for you. We as humans learn better, and retain information more when we hear stories. How do we tell good stories?

If you've ever seen a movie, then you have a basic understanding of the story telling process. The movie starts out introducing the audience to a certain time and place, where our main character is currently existing. We get to know a little bit about that character and find out they yearn for something. Then they decide to go on this journey to get something that they desire to have. There's some struggle along the way, things don't come easy, conflict helps the story become more interesting. Then they get what they wanted, have a big conflict about it, before they return home, having had a huge transformation from the journey.

I'll give you an example with one of my all-time favorite movies, Nacho Libre. The story starts off with Nacho, a Mexican monk that was orphaned and grew up in a monastery, running around the monastery with a Luchador mask. It's clear right away that he doesn't fit in and his biggest desire is to be a Luchador (wrestler). Unfortunately, it's not okay for a monk to be a wrestler, so Nacho had to be very secretive in his pursuit of becoming one. He recruits a partner, creates his costume and competes in many wrestling matches, losing almost every single one. He's eventually discovered by his fellow monks at the monastery and is outcasted to the wilderness. Luckily he finds out he qualifies for a huge match that will cement him as a professional wrestler and help him save enough money to make his home better for all of the orphans he takes care of. So he competes in the match and fights his heart out and is victorious! In the end he's able to go back to the monastery a hero and transform it for the better. Nacho went from a disrespected monk with kitchen duty to a leader and hero at his monastery by following his dreams and becoming a Luchador.

It's simple enough, all stories have a beginning, a middle and an end. Check out some fairy tales and study their format. "Once upon a time, something, something, something, and they lived happily ever after." Below I've put together a little bit of a formula to help you tell a clear and concise story for your posts. Russel Brunson came up with a lot of this after talking to the creator of the movie Hitch and learning about the framework of what makes a good movie.

The Easy Story Formula

1. **Where does the story start/What's going on? (Describe backstory, your feelings)**

2. **What did you want to achieve/have?**

3. **Why couldn't you have/achieve that?**

4. **So what did you do about it/What journey did you go on?**

5. **Did you pay a hefty price or come into conflict?**

6. **What transformation did you go through?**

You literally just need to answer these questions before you tell your story. Once you do, you'll have a story that has all the details it needs and none of the rambling some of us are really good at. You can use this formula on most if not all of your pieces of content, even when you're teaching something, (which we'll talk about a little later). It's universal and will help you tell some really good stories. So start with your origin story, then find things that happen to you in everyday life to pull stories from.

A great way to keep track of stories in your life is to carry a notebook around with you. When something happens write it down so you can remember it later. Another great tip I got from my mentors was to write down all of your biggest moments in your business and create stories from those moments. Your journey probably wasn't easy; you probably went through a lot just to get to where you are now. People want to know about it!

Show the world there's no such thing as an overnight success! Document your work! By documenting your journey, you're literally creating endless amounts of content. You are showing people exactly what you are doing and they get to see it all in real time. You're also building up a huge database of content so when no matter where people discover you on your journey, they can look back and see where it all started.

I'm doing this right now with my podcast, "Brimo Live Journey To 6 Figures." I'm documenting my journey to six figures, with the wins, the losses and interviewing fellow digital marketers so that other people can get the inside look of what I'm doing. I want people to see that not only is it possible but that I'm achieving it while they get a front row seat.

What I also love about doing my podcast, is all the interviews with my friends. Collaborations are such an easy and great way to create content. One of my videos that had a lot of views did so because I was partnered with a local organization. I am a huge animal lover! When I found out that our local animal shelter was rolling out a program called Shelter Paws, where you can rent a dog for a day, I knew my wife and I had to sign up! Shelter dogs get a bad rap and I knew that this program could help a lot of dogs get adopted so I made sure to document our experience. When we got to the shelter we got to select one of the eligible pups from their kennel in the back. We walked around for a few minutes until we happened upon this Jack Russell mix named Henry. He was black and white, very quiet but came up to us in his kennel.

Once we got through the processing part of checking him out, we took him on a nice little trip. We stopped at Lowe's so he could gander at all the home improvement wares while also smelling everything in sight, and it was cute filming him walking down the aisles there. Then we made sure to get him a pupuccino at Starbucks. It's just a fancy name for a cup of whip cream but most dogs LOVE it! Then we stopped at Petsmart so he could check out the toy aisle. My favorite part of this was there at Petsmart when Henry was in the toy aisle. He was sniffing the toys curiously until he happened upon one he really liked. Then he proceeded to start playing with it right there in front of us. It was the cutest thing! And it became the highlight of the video I made of him and our day.

Once I edited the video I posted it on Facebook and tagged the animal shelter. Within a few days I had over 6,000 views and quite a few shares as well. Henry had gone viral here in San Antonio and it was because I had utilized the followers of the shelter to spread his video around. This is an easy way to get more followers or views on your content.

If you have colleagues in the same industry or similar industry, you can partner up and create an incredible piece of content. Whether it's a video, podcast episode, or anything else amazing, you both have something you can use and leverage each other's audiences to build awareness.

On the topic of collaboration, you've also got the chance to do joint ventures. You can partner with that same person and create an incredible offer that would cater to both of your audiences. Talk about conversions! (We will a little later on in this book). You can also put together contests which followers love! You can partner up with a few others, everybody chips in $50-$100 and you can either collectively purchase a high ticket item, like a camera, gift basket, etc, or you can put it on one giftcard for Visa or Amazon, and give it away to the winners of the contest. This will help you grow your following and also reach more people. You have everyone that wants to enter, like the post, follow all the contributors, and comment with tagging one of their friends below. This particular approach works better on Instagram because Facebook doesn't like ads that tell people to like/comment/tag their friends unfortunately. You can do it on your personal profile no problem, (at least as this book is being written) but you can't run ads or boost the post.

I've also put together a cheatsheet for coming up with endless ideas. That way instead of scrambling for ideas all the time, you can find a topic and post about it quickly. But once you've been posting content for a while, it gets easier. You build momentum and it becomes second nature to post amazing stuff to your social media. Get out there and start creating! The more consistent you can get with creating content, the better. I promise you once it becomes a habit you'll barely have to think about it. But another hack to consistent content is to pre-schedule all of your content in advance.

I use a site called buffer.com. It's super easy and you can have three social media accounts for free. One day a week you can spend a couple of hours just scheduling content. Then everyday something is going to publish on your social media site while you're out living your life. How awesome is that?!

Don't forget about things that are going on in the world right now. It's important to stay relevant to today's culture because you can easily be forgotten if you don't. A good place to check out what's trending right now is buzzsumo.com. Here you'll find tons of topics that are trending in a wide variety of industries. So if you're struggling to stay up to date on what's going on, then cruise this site for a bit until you find something good. Twitter also has it's "what's trending section", here you can see what people are talking about and join the conversation.

It's okay to share other people's work as long as you credit them. They'll probably appreciate it, and you can potentially build a relationship with them which is always a good business idea. You want as many friends in your space as possible, because you can go a lot further with more contacts. We already talked about how powerful joint ventures can be. When you help others they'll be more than happy to return the favor usually, so make a lot of friends!

Once we've built up an audience, and we're already getting the hang of content creation, it's important to know what your audience's specific needs are. Content isn't just a personal experience, it's educational and it helps provide solutions. That's how we can start ringing that money bell. People will appreciate getting to know you, but they'll like you even more when your product and services make their lives better. So if you haven't done research to see what they're looking for, then do it now!

The next page is your Content Creation Cheatsheet! Use this to come up with endless content ideas, especially if you ever find yourself stuck and out of ideas. Remember that constantly learning is a great way to keep that content flow coming. In the next chapter we'll talk more about figuring out your ideal customers' needs and connecting with your audience.

CHEATSHEET.
1. Tell a good story
2. What are you working on right now?

3. What's going on in your life/business?
4. What are you learning?
5. What are you reading?
6. What's a good life hack you have?
7. Ask a question to your audience
8. Do a Facebook live
9. What random national holiday is it?
10. Ask me anything live/post
11. Share a good memory
12. What are you currently launching/offering?
13. Post a funny gif
14. Go do something new and then talk about it
15. Go out into nature
16. Spend time with people you care about
17. Show off your pets
18. Ask for recommendations (books, shows, etc.)
19. Give a tip for something you're good at
20. Go on vacation
21. What was your most recent purchase?
22. Tell a joke
23. Do a giveaway
24. Share a win

Chapter 5 Connecting with Your Audience

In 2014 I made an "It Gets Better Video" on one of my YouTube channels. For those of you who are unaware of what an "It Gets Better Video" is, it's a video that older LGBTQIA people make for LGBTQIA youth that are struggling with bullying, homophobia from their family or people in their lives, or all together just going through a rough time because of who they are. I myself struggled for years with being gay, because I was raised in a very conservative church that was not accepting of LGBTQIA individuals.

I went through a big journey of accepting myself and keeping my faith in God. I left the church that I was extremely involved in, I disconnected with friends that didn't accept my "lifestyle" and only hung around people that accepted me for all of me. In the process I read a lot of books, watched a lot of documentaries, and talked to people that had gone through similar experiences with being gay and Christian.

After all of it I was able to love and appreciate myself for who I felt God created me to be and I wanted to share my experience with LGBTQIA youth that struggled with the same thing. So I made my "It Gets Better Video" and just let it run.

Back then I didn't know much about SEO, video ranking, or going viral. So for a while I didn't see many results and got discouraged. I almost forgot about it until two years later, when I decided to check the old email account associated with that YouTube channel. To my surprise I had two teens reach out to me about my video and asking for my help. In those two years I had moved from Texas to California and one of the teens lived in a neighboring town to the city I lived in.

I responded back to him and we began a conversation which ultimately led to us meeting up at a coffee shop in downtown Long Beach. His name was Nick and he had come out as gay and was having issues with his family and church accepting him for who he was. He had gone through a lot of depression and even contemplated suicide. But somehow he stumbled across my video and he told me that it helped save his life.

When I first made that video I was hoping to reach a bunch of youth that could benefit from it. But I also wanted to build up a huge following like some of the other LGBTQIA influencers I had seen before. When I didn't get the results I wanted right away I stepped away from it and didn't stay consistent with posting content. But meeting Nick and getting emails from him and the other teen, made me realize that there were so many more gratifying results than just building up a huge following.

Helping someone decide not to end their life because of a video I made feels so much more amazing than if I had a bunch of subscribers who I may not have necessarily impacted. It was important for me to make that video because I was able to help someone, but it was even more important for me to reach out to those that emailed me after seeing my video, because it showed that I cared enough about what they were going through.

We talked about this a little bit in the last chapter, but I want to drive home how important it is for you to continue that conversation with your audience. I don't care if you have 5 followers or 5 million followers, if you're not answering some of their comments, questions, or taking any of their feedback, then they will lose respect for you very quickly. If you only have a handful of followers then you have a duty to reply to every single comment.

When Gary Vaynerchuk was just getting started, he would stay up until 2 am answering comments, messages, and questions his followers had. He understood how big it was to be personable and to show how much he cared for his followers. That's why he not only blew up so big, but also why his fans are some of the most loyal you'll see anywhere. So be personable, be authentic and continue the conversation.

Your fans will appreciate the time you took to listen to them. Especially when they give you feedback on your content. They are the biggest gauge to whether or not your content is awesome or if it sucks a big one. Your content is created for them, not for you. Let me repeat that, it is about them not you! It's important that you take their opinions into account when it comes to what you post on social media. If you give them a ton of value, they'll love you for it and buy everything you put out. But if all you do is sell them things because you're concerned about how much money you can make, then you're never going to get anywhere. People talk, so if you piss off enough of them, you won't get followers easily.

Take examples from brands that are big on customer service. Zappos is one of the best examples of customer service that goes above and beyond to make sure their customers are happy. There was a rumor going around once, that Zappos even ordered a pizza for a client. Talk about customer service! A shoe company ordering someone a pizza? Zappos ensures that all of their employees understand that their brand is about providing great products, and making sure they're doing all they can for their customers. If you want to do well, then pay attention to your customers' needs and make them happy. You go a lot further in life by the way you serve people.

Also, don't be fake. People can sniff out BS a mile away so you might as well be real when you communicate. The truth will come out eventually. Recently a viral video called out life advice guru, Jay Shetty. The video said that he was taking famous quotes and putting his name at the end of them as if he said them himself. That's plagiarism and it can get you into a lot of trouble. It just made him look like a fraud and people lost respect for him when they saw that. So don't lie about anything, the truth is always the best route to take.

I talked about being authentic earlier, but I really want you to get this point. Show some of your vulnerability to your following. You don't have to tell every single life story, but you do have to open up a little bit about who you are and what you stand for. I told the world about my experience as a gay teen and what I went through. Because of that I've helped at least two people and made a life-long friend out of it. This all happened when I decided to be vulnerable in front of my audience.

If you need an example of what vulnerability looks like, take a note from Brene' Brown's TED talk. Just go to YouTube and type in "Brene Brown TED Talk." Brown epitomizes the idea of vulnerable when she talks about her journey of figuring out what vulnerability really is. Like most of us, she first thought that being vulnerable was a sign of weakness. By doing vast amounts of research on the subject, she discovered that, being vulnerable is one of the strongest acts of courage anyone could perform.

Her talk is inspiring, eye opening, and you guessed it, vulnerable. She received a standing ovation from the crowd, her talk is one of the most viewed TED Talks of all time, and she's a best-selling author. Being vulnerable is the key to really connecting with your audience, and when you're brave enough to share what's on your heart, you'll resonate with people and amazing results can happen.

Again this is about being REAL. Not making up some sob story to get likes and shares. We are here to help make the world a better place with our products, services and even our content. So allow yourself to be open, and also figure out what message you want people to hear. Your message aligns with your story and your values. Your content allows you to share that message with those that will get value out of hearing it.

Your message comes from your life experiences and the knowledge you've gained a long your journey. My message (from my YouTube video), was that even if you're going through a rough time because of who you are, things will eventually get better. You just have to hold on and keep moving forward. I conveyed that message by telling the story of what I went through figuring myself out and the things that I experienced along the road to self-acceptance.

So really think about the messages you want to send with your posts and how it's going to help your ideal audience. Put yourself in their shoes and think about the conversations they may be having in their own head. They've got problems in their lives, how can you help fix those problems? It all comes down to the six basic human needs.

Chapter 6 Psych 101

Now before we get into everybody's favorite part (money), you've got to learn a little bit about what makes a human tick. We are all wired with basic human wants and needs that have evolved from when humans first appeared, but we still have a lot of the same instincts as our ancestors. When you understand these basic human traits, then you can really communicate your message to your audience a lot easier than if you didn't. I will say that this chapter is not intended to manipulate people in any way, shape, or form. My intention is to help you help more people not to manipulate anybody. So if you're intention is to hurt people for your own benefit…then feel free to read a different book.

Our brains are literally a work of art. They have evolved and adapted, allowing our species to survive thousands of years on this planet and it's incredible! Yet even with our incredible ability to adapt and change, the basics of what we need and desire haven't really changed much at all. There are six basic human wants and needs and they are as follows:

1. Safety

2. Survival

3. Security

4. Sustenance

5. Sex

6. Status

When you begin to understand how humans tick, you can begin to understand how to help fulfill their needs. When you can help, you can build trust and gain respect for your brand. These needs are naturally engrained in our brains. It's literally what our brain is seeking out day in and day out to keep us alive. I think they're self-explanatory but let's get into it a little bit.

1. Safety – As humans we naturally look for shelter from the storms of life. We need housing to protect us from weather and other dangers. We have alarm systems, guard dogs, and cameras. Keeping ourselves and our assets safe is something we care passionately about and spend quite a bit of money on.

2. Survival – We're all focused on staying alive! "Look both ways before crossing the street." "Put your seatbelt on in the car." "Make sure your food is cooked thoroughly before eating it." We have rules that we follow in order to protect ourselves from danger. Staying alive is our biggest prerogative. When we're alive we're able to fulfill all of the other needs we have and live the life we desire.

3. Security – All of these precautions that we take to keep us safe and alive, bring us the peace of mind that we are secure. We want to feel safe, we want to be protected and know that everything's going to be alright. Everyone is striving for financial security, but they also want everything else to be secure as well. We like knowing that everything is going to be alright.

4. Sustenance – We have to have food in order to survive. Our diets dictate our health and well-being. We were made to eat so that we could energize our bodies to live. The food gives us nutrients which literally help our bodies function properly. So sustenance is huge!

5. Sex – The human race has survived so long because of our ability to reproduce offspring. We all have the desire inside of us to have sex, it's natural (nothing to be afraid of), and it's pertinent for our species to survive for future generations.

6. Status – We all want to fit in with our peers. Back during the hunter-gatherer phases, humans lived in tribes. In the tribes they relied on each other to survive. So being ostracized from the group meant you were almost guaranteed to die. Sometimes it still feels like that when you don't fit in.

When you study the six basic human needs, you start to understand the mind and motivations of every single human being on the planet. Yes, we're all different in a lot of ways, but we're all the same in others. We need these six basic needs met in order to live happy healthy lives. It goes deep into our DNA.

These are the reasons people will buy your product, listen to your message or want to follow you. When you can help people with any of these needs you're helping fulfill things that people are already searching for answers to. It makes it a lot easier to get your stuff out to the right audience as well.

This obviously has more to do with marketing and selling, but it can also be used with content creation. All content creation really is, is marketing for your brand. I recommend studying the most effective Superbowl commercials and discovering what made them work so well. What needs did they speak to? Why were they so memorable? Companies spend millions of dollars on those commercials and some completely flop, while others are memorable, but not all of them get people to buy.

To learn more about what goes on inside of our brains and how effective it is in marketing I highly recommend the book Unconscious Branding by Douglas Van Praet. Douglas is a world class marketer that's worked for some of the most well-known brands in the world. He understands what drives people to buy better than anyone I know. I couldn't put his book down when I read it and it'll help you even more when you start creating campaigns.

For now, I just wanted you to have a basic understanding of what drives people so as you start building your brand and consistently creating your content, you'd have a leg up above the competition. The better you understand what makes human tick, the better you can communicate with them and show them why you're the best person to help them fulfill those needs.

Chapter 7 How to Start Monetizing

If you haven't already, then you should create a customer avatar of what your ideal client would look like. How old are they? What do they do for a living? Are they married or single? How much education do they have? Do they have children? Do they own or rent their home? What is their income range? When you know the answers to these questions, then you are ready to figure out exactly what they need help with.

The easiest way to figure out what your prospect's problems are is to ask them. Join different groups on social media and see what they're talking about. A great resource for that is Quora.com. It's an online forum where people can ask questions and others will answer it for them. You can post polls in groups or on your social media pages and have your audience answer questions. Also see what they've previously commented on your other posts. You have to do some research in your market if you want to create offers that will best serve their needs.

If you don't have an offer, then you're not ready to convert. If you do have an offer you can skip ahead a little bit while I catch the rest of the class up with crafting irresistible offers. There's a reason why I didn't use product/service instead of the offer. There's a big difference between just your product/service and an irresistible offer. An offer includes your product/service but also adds so much value that the cost of everything (your price) looks so low that the buyer would be crazy not to jump in! Remember those digital assets I was talking about earlier? Now is when those are going to come in handy.

A good example would be if you were to go to a restaurant and they told you that they had a "Date Night Special." It would be two salads, two entrees, a bottle of wine, and dessert all for the price of only $50. That's an irresistible offer for someone wanting to spoil their significant other but also not wanting to break the bank. A nice dinner can cost at least $50, and that's before the wine. So what can you add to your course, book, service, whatever you have, that you're selling?

If you're still stuck, then I highly recommend doing what Russel Brunson does and funnel-hacking someone in the same industry as you. You can find tons of offers at a site like clickbank.com. Find one that's similar to yours and see what their funnel and offer looks like. Now don't copy everything, including the offer because that's immoral, but get ideas that can help you create the kind of offer people just can't wait to buy!

Now that you have that incredible offer, it's time to start using your content to draw in the right people. You've already established some of the problems that your audience wants to be solved, so take that list and start creating videos, podcast episodes, blogs, or whatever your chosen social media platform utilizes, and start educating them on how they can solve the problem.

An easy way to position your content is to follow these steps here:
1. Call out your prospective client by starting your post with "If you" or "do you"
2. Talk about their problem or their desired outcome (example: "If you have back pain")
3. Show them how to solve their problem/achieve their desired outcome
4. Present your offer
5. Tell them how to get it (Call to Action)

This will help you start getting people interested in what you have to offer. Utilize this type of content frequently because you're providing value by showing them how to fix their problem, but also allowing them to go deeper with you in your offer. If you do a good job, you'll start getting people to go to your website, landing page, or wherever you're sending them with your call to action, (The call to action tells them what to do, click here, call me, etc.). Only have one call to action in your piece of content, because a confused mind will always say no. So only tell them to do one thing at a time. I like this approach because at the very beginning you're calling out the people who this piece of content will help so it qualifies them in the beginning. It's great to get leads but it's not so great if they don't even qualify for what you're offering because they won't buy. So this approach helps you weed out the ones who don't qualify right away.

By this point you should already have started posting content regularly so add in at least one of these types of posts (video, podcast, blog) a week to drive that traffic. You can do this organically from your personal profile. I made $400 in 21 days by posting a Facebook Live every day on my personal profile and pitching an offer I was promoting at the time. At the time I probably had around 1000-1500 friends on Facebook. I didn't use any ads so it was pure profit. I didn't pitch every single day, but I did it enough to get that four hundred bucks and I was happy about that. Just think of all the results I could've gotten if I would have been using paid ads.

Once you've got some ad budget, I highly recommend doing some paid ads on your social media platform. If you have no idea how to post an ad on Facebook, Instagram, Pinterest, or any other platform then get over to our good friend YouTube and look up how to place an ad. As a marketer everything is a test, so you won't know what's going to work until you try it out. By posting new content all the time you'll start to notice what works with your audience and what doesn't. Paid ads not only give you a lot more reach, but they also tell you what works and what doesn't a lot quicker than organic traffic.

If you own a business, then you NEED to start utilizing paid traffic because you're losing money if you don't. You have an irresistible offer already, so you might as well get as many people in front of it as possible. Right now social media advertising is the cheapest it's ever going to be, so I encourage you to get in front of the curve and start using it.

I also recommend always plugging your links in as many places as possible. So for example on YouTube, you have a description box underneath your video. Whether you have a call to action in your video or not (which you should because people need to be told what to do to get them to buy), you can post a link to your offer. On Instagram, for a lot of my posts I'll put my username @brimomorales, so that it reminds people who I am and where they can find me. By dropping links in as many places as you can, you never know when a sale can come in. Most of your social media profiles will have a place for you to put your website link up already, so make sure it's there and also utilize it in your posts where you're able to. Make it as easy for people to buy from you as possible.

I'll also give you some advice on attracting customers to you. This is not a sales book by any means but I think having some sales knowledge is extremely beneficial for any business. The best thing you can do is learn how to be appealing to your audience instead of repelling them like the plague. The first tip I would give you is to get to know your customers' needs and wants. When you go shopping for a new car and the salesman only wants to show you the latest model, the bells and whistles, the shallow stuff that doesn't suit your needs, the last thing you'll want to do is sign on the dotted line. Instead you'll walk right out of there and probably never come back. It was obvious the salesman was only concerned about how big of a commission he could get, instead of meeting your needs. So don't do this to your clients! I'll tell you a story of when a salesman made me want to run for the hills. One day I was browsing at Best Buy, I wanted to price some DSLR camera's and was looking at a model I heard a lot about. This young salesman, maybe 23 or so, saw me hunched over the camera, toggling the buttons and things. "Oh I see you're looking at the Lumix GH5, this is a really powerful camera. I would know because I went to school for video, and I do freelance on the side". "Oh I guess that's not going very good for you then…" Just kidding! I didn't say that to him, I just thought it. Instead I informed him that I was just looking and didn't need any help. He rather repulsed me by coming on so strong, I didn't ask for his resume, I just wanted to check out a camera. The moral of the story is, don't come on like a sleaze, take an interest in your audience.

Show them that you care (as I've said many times before), by getting to know their needs and desires. Let's look at the car dealership scenario again, but this time the salesman puts you first. You walk into the car dealership, he greets you with a nice smile, he asks you what it is you're looking for in a car. What's important to you? Is it safety? Reliability? Do you want Bluetooth so you can hook up your phone and listen to your latest podcast? He'll learn because he took the time to get to know you and what your needs were. Because of that, you left happy with your new car, and he felt good for helping you. We want to create as many win/win situations as we can. Helping people will not only make you feel good but it'll grow your wallet, and I know that's something you'll be happy about. My mentors have told me that the amount of money you make is based on the amount of value you bring to the world. So start helping as many people as you can!

My next piece of advice for attracting customers is to work on not being desperate for sales. People can smell desperation a mile away. Just think back to a time when a guy or girl was crazy desperate to get your attention. You may have thought it was nice that you were getting attention for a minute but not long after you realized how desperate they were, you ran for the hills! I'm guilty of avoiding any of those salespeople at the mall that try to get you to check out their hair straighteners or lotions. They thrive on sales and are desperate to make them. Don't be like that.

Instead just be extremely passionate about your offer because you know how much it's going to help them change their life. It's your duty to help people with what you have, so why not do your due diligence of getting it into the hands of as many people as possible? Again this is not desperation, this is being on fire for your product because you use it yourself and can't help but to tell everybody about it. Nobody wants to hear a sales pitch but everyone appreciates a good product tip from a friend. One of my favorite books is You Are a Badass at Making Money by Jen Sincero, and I will tell everybody that'll listen to me, about it. This book changed my life and helped me write this book you're reading now. So if you want a book to help you change the way you think about money, and possibly make a little more, then go get that book! You're welcome.

That's an example of being passionate about your stuff, you want to tell everybody about it because you know how powerful it is, you're walking proof!

Another piece of advice would be, never sell anything you're not going to use yourself. People can tell when you're being inauthentic and if you can't vouch for a product because you don't even use it, then why should someone else buy from you? It just doesn't work like that. That's why I can't jump into a lot of those MLM gigs. I don't want to use those products and I don't want to bother my friends and family. If I were to pitch those products that vibe would come off and I would fail to sell anything.

If you're in an MLM situation, know that the information in this book can help you stop bothering your friends and family and bring it all online to where people that want your products are hanging out. I know of people that are super successful with MLMs because they're utilizing social media and online marketing. It's possible and if I were into that I would be doing it too. I do utilize funnels in my marketing though and in the next chapter I'm going to explain funnels a little more in-depth.

Chapter 8 The Funnel

The funnel has been the secret weapon to how I was able to start making an income online. My mentor taught me how to build funnels and start my own online business from scratch. When I first started learning this stuff, I had no idea what a funnel was or how it worked. Once I got the concept down and started learning how to put all the pieces together, I realized how incredibly powerful funnels could be.

I distinctly remember making my first sale online and how good it felt! I was still working my full-time job and had stepped outside. I felt my phone vibrate in my pocket, I had gotten an email. I opened it up to find that I had made my first sale! It was surreal! I put together this thing online and it was making money for me! This is how a lot of people can break away from their full-time jobs and work for themselves.

So if you don't have a sales funnel together I highly recommend that you build one. A sales funnel is a series of webpages that sell your offers for you. It's like having a salesperson working for you 24/7. You may have even gotten this book from a funnel. It can start from a simple ad placed on social media. It could say something like, "free book shows you how to stand out on social media just pay for shipping." So you clicked on the ad and it sent you to a page that said "Fill out this form with your info to get your book." This is called a landing page or a squeeze page, where you put in your billing and shipping info so that the book comes to you. This is how we're able to gather potential client's information. The landing page is where you offer something in exchange for their information, in this case, it's my book.

After you put in your shipping information, the next page is usually another offer of some sort, maybe even an upsell (a slightly higher offer or an add on to the original offer). A funnel can have multiple offers but I wouldn't put more than 3 or 4 into one funnel. If you do that, you risk upsetting the customer and then they won't want to buy from you in the future. Our job is to make the buying process fun while meeting the needs of the customers at the same time.

Once they get passed your landing page, they'll have given you their information. If you've set your funnel up correctly, that means that they're now on your email list. You can now email them special offers in the future to rake in more sales. I've been told that an email list is one of the most valuable things a marketer can have, and I honestly believe that's the case. If you are doing a great job of providing amazing content and offers, then you will have a list of raving fans that can't wait to keep buying from you. Some will even buy every single offer you put out because they've benefited from your offers in the past. This is a great position to be in! This is also where I hope you'll end up by trying out everything I've taught you so far in this book.

Building funnels can seem like a daunting task and if it sounds like more than you can handle there's nothing wrong with finding someone to do it for you. Funnel Rolodex is a great place to find funnel builders and you can check that out by going to www.funnelrolodex.com.

There's plenty of funnel builders ready and waiting to build up that perfect funnel for your offers. It's not difficult for you to build your funnel though, and if you'd like to try it out for yourself then you can get a two-week free trial of the website where I build all of my funnels by going to https://go.brimagraphics.com/clickfunnels and signing up. They have plenty of templates for you to choose from so you don't have to build it all from scratch. They even have tutorial videos to help you out along the way. No matter what method you go about building your funnel, just make sure you get it built so that you can then put the link to your funnel in as many places as possible.

You can create a funnel for any type of business, niche, or offer. There are so many different types of funnels and I can't go into all of them because that could be another book in itself. A few examples are funnels that take a person through a webinar, sales video, or even an application. You can utilize the funnel for building a newsletter list, leads for real estate, and whatever else you can imagine. Your funnel may come to be your secret weapon to monetizing your content as well.

After reading this book, I highly encourage you to start creating that incredible content I've been talking about. The content that will attract your ideal customer. They'll get to know you, they'll like you, and they'll trust you because you've helped them before you've sold them anything. Once you've put out some value, then add your link (to your funnel or website) into your content so that your fans can see your amazing offer! Then the money will start rolling in. It really can be that simple.

It's not going to happen overnight, it's not going to be the easiest thing you've ever done, but I promise you it will be so worth it! Whether you touch one life, ten lives or 10,000 lives, you will have made an impact in this world and that's something you can be incredibly proud of. This is my vision for you and the reason that I've taken the time to write this book. So I encourage you to take action on this and put forth the effort because you might just find that your goals actually get accomplished.

Chapter 9 What Makes Content Go Viral?

I want to start this chapter off by saying that there is no guarantee that a video or other piece of content, will go viral. A lot of the time it's a happy coincidence. Like the Chewbacca mom who's laugh was so contagious her video just had to be shared. I'm sure when she shot that live video from her van in the Kohl's parking lot, she had no idea it would be shared thousands of times by people all over the world. But you can do your best to create quality content that provides value to people, is entertaining, and makes your audience feel good. That's how a video can potentially go viral.

I listened to a podcast recently with Jay Shetty, if you don't know who he is look him up on Facebook. He does a great job making his videos go viral. He teaches the wisdom he learned from becoming a Buddhist monk at a young age and tells stories on topics in his videos. There's almost always actors portraying what he's saying and he's gotten a rhythm and timing down that only comes with producing so many videos over time. People like the positivity and the hope he brings to the world. Jay touched on five different types of emotions that tend to go viral so I wanted to talk about those here. They are, comedy, emotional, inspirational, adventure, and surprise.

Obviously Chewbacca mom falls under the comedy section, but don't worry if you're not naturally funny or feel that it would be hard for you to make funny content on purpose. You don't have to, there are four other emotions you can play around with as well.

Emotional doesn't necessarily mean sad by the way. Emotional means that the video made you feel something. A great example would be one of those dodo videos where a dog comes from a really bad situation and then goes through an amazing transformation. You watch every step of the journey and feel like you're right along with the dog. So when you see them come out happy on the other side you're just full of all "the feels." You laughed, you cried, you went through the entire spectrum practically.

Inspirational is pretty easy to understand. It can be similar to the dog video of going through a transformation, but inspirational makes you feel like you can take on the world and dominate. It encourages you to be your best person and make a difference, you're literally "inspired" to take action.

Adventure is equal to any of those videos we see of people doing incredible stunts, traveling the world, or doing something out of the ordinary that catches our attention. It makes us awe in wonder and cringe at the peril of what "might happen" to whoever is in the video.

Surprise is when you're watching a video and then all of a sudden it takes a completely different turn. A great example of surprise is all those videos that came out in the early 2000s where you had to stare at the screen and look for something, only to have a scary face pop out at you at the end. I remember quite a few America's Funniest Home Video's episodes with people watching those videos and it was hilarious. That's just one example, but surprise keeps your audience engaged because as they're watching they're unsure of what will happen next. You keep the video moving and make it exciting for them with unexpected outcomes.

Positive emotions make us feel good and we like to share things that put us in that happy state. This is why I like these five emotions when it comes to producing viral content. When you stick with the other spectrum of the emotional wheel, like anger, sadness, you probably won't find as much luck with people sharing your content. Anger will rile people up and you may get some shares that way, but I almost guarantee that by sticking with the happier emotions you'll gain a lot more traction and have more of your content getting closer to going viral.

Also just study other videos that have gone viral. Do any of them relate to your message? What aspects made them get so much attention? What emotions do they fall into as described earlier in this chapter? By studying content, you'll be able to find patterns for going viral that'll help you with your content as well.

Another way to go viral is to collaborate with someone that already has a fairly big following. My wife and I participated in a program called Shelter Paws at our animal shelter in town. For a day we could go in and take a dog out of the shelter to spoil him and hope to get attention so he could be adopted. Me, being the marketer that I am, filmed the experience and created a video to showcase his personality and all the fun we had. His name was Henry by the way, and he totally stole the show.

Once the day was up and we took him back to the shelter, I edited the video and posted it onto Facebook and tagged the shelter. They shared the video and in less than a week we already had over 6,000+ views. I did not pay for a single ad for that video to get viewed and so many people saw it and shared it because they were already following the animal shelter. So I leveraged their following without even trying to, I just wanted people to see how awesome Henry was so he could get adopted.

So if you know of anyone that already has a decent-sized following see how you can help them and how you can collaborate to create something that will benefit both of your audiences. It's a great way to gain visibility quickly and collaborating is a lot of fun! It's also usually a win/win. Just make sure you have a quality offer because if you don't it'll backfire on you quickly in front of someone else's audience.

The fastest and easiest way to go viral though is to do paid ads. I've easily gotten over 10-20,000 views on videos for really cheap by using paid ads. It's a great way to get exposure and to see what types of people like your content. So why not invest in your content so that you can help more people? You're missing out if you don't. If you're unsure about how to go about placing ads on social media, then head over to my website https://go.brimagraphics.com/web-reg and discover some strategies on making it happen.

Becoming viral is not a guarantee, and you may envision something as going viral and plan for it, but then it could be a huge flop. You can't be married to just one idea when it comes to content. So knowing that not every piece will do well, helps you to become good at testing.

Just like scientists, good marketers understand the scientific process. You come up with a hypothesis, (an idea for a piece of content and the outcome you'd like to have) and you test it out to see if it works or not. The fastest way to test is with ads because you'll reach a bunch of people in a short amount of time. From there you'll see if they are engaging, sharing, or subscribing to your page.

Decide what type of outcome you'd like to come from your content. Are you growing your page? Do you want people to share and engage? Do you want to drive people to your website to become clients? This is going to assist you with your testing and the settings you use for your ads. I'm not going to get into how to place the ads technically because the ad platforms change constantly and I want this book to be relevant for a long time. You should know at least a little about one ad platform now, but if you need more assistance then head over to https://go.brimagraphics.com/web-reg. You'll be able to jump into one of the most comprehensive courses in digital marketing, which includes the Facebook ad platform.

Once you know what you want with your content you're going to make a few variations of it. If you're using pictures then consider different pictures with the same text (copy), all going to the same audience. Or use the same picture and text for a handful of different audiences. If you're using a video, then test out different audiences and the headline. You'll never know what works amazingly unless you test everything. If you already have a huge following, then testing is a little easier because you already have raving fans that know you well enough to give you honest feedback. If they like your stuff they'll share it, engage with it, and buy your product. If your stuff sucks they'll tell you and they won't do what you want them to.

Once you do have a big following, it's important to continue to grow your audience from time to time. Don't become complacent because you never know when someone will just up and decide to stop following you. Keep the conversation going and keep producing amazing content so your earlier subscribers still love you, and new subscribers discover you all the time. Paid traffic helps you do all of this at a reasonably low cost.

If for some reason you're completely against using paid advertising, know that it's still possible to be successful but you'll just go at a much slower rate. You've also got to understand that what you won't spend in money will be spent on time. You'll have to create a lot of content, post constantly and pray that people will see it. What's a better return on your investment? I'd go with some sort of paid strategy so that you could save time and frustration.

If you're short on money look into creative ways to build an ad budget. I have a podcast episode of easy ways to making $100 in a short amount of time that you can check out by going to brimomorales.com That'll give you some ideas into creating a budget to get you started. You've invested in yourself to get this book, and you've invested in your future by making it this far into the book, don't stop now. You could create something truly amazing with way less the cost of starting a traditional business.

Chapter 10 Hashtags and Keywords

You'll know by now if your particular social media platform uses hashtags or not. I talked about it briefly when I spoke about all of the different social media sites in chapter one, but I think they deserve their very own chapter because you can do so many things with hashtags. The premise of hashtags is very similar to keywords for SEO.

If you're unfamiliar with SEO, it stands for search engine optimization. This helps your website, blog, or landing page appear higher in search engines like Google, Yahoo!, or Bing. The higher your website, the more likely someone is to click on it. So being ranked highly is very much to your advantage. With SEO, it works a lot with keywords, these are words people are already searching for. Think of the last time you used Google to search for something. If you're looking for sushi restaurants, chances are you typed something in like "sushi near me." This is how keywords work. With your videos, blogs, and hashtags, you'll use phrases people are already searching for.

I pointed out earlier that Twitter has its own "Trending Hashtags" section, this is a great place to stay on top of what's happening in the world. By seeing what people are already talking about, you can easily jump in on the conversation and post relevant content. That's an incredible ability! I don't expect you to keep up with everything everyone's talking about, but there are plenty of topics for you to jump into that also have to do with your business or niche.

Just like with SEO, your posts can be seen first when they start to get a lot of engagement. On Twitter, people have the option of liking your posts, retweeting, and responding. The more engagement you can get, the higher your post will appear in the newsfeed. You'll want to use hashtags in your posts, finding out which ones are already working is the way to go, especially when you're new to social media.

Instagram has a very similar way of using hashtags. You can search hashtags and it'll show you how many posts there are with that hashtag. When you search for or select a particular hashtag, the most engaging posts will show up first, just like on Twitter. On Instagram you can use up to 30 hashtags. The more hashtags you use, the more categories your post will fall into. I like using all 30 when I can. Some of my mentors have even suggested that a combination of super-popular hashtags and somewhat less popular hashtags is the best way to go. The fewer people that use a certain hashtag, the more chance you have of ranking higher and more people seeing that post. So don't shy away from a hashtag just because it's been used less than 100,000 times.

  Hashtags are a great way to get exposure, and trend into what's already popular. It works over a multitude of social media sites, so you need to have at least a little bit of understanding about how it all works. Depending on when you're reading this book, hashtags may or may not be around anymore, but SEO and keywords will be. So will the idea of wanting your content to show up first when someone is searching for a particular topic or keyword.

  Don't be afraid to utilize hashtags or to purposefully put in keywords relating to your content that people are already searching for. This is the easiest way to utilize SEO and to get your content to be seen in such a busy place. Utilize as many of these strategies in this book as you possibly can, so that your content will perform better, your message will be heard, and you can be paid for the amazing services that you are providing to the world.

Chapter 11 Maximize Your Content Quickly

Now that you've got some understanding on how to create effective content, it's time to take your training to the next level. Content is key when it comes to growing your following, building your credibility, and of course driving sales. So the more you can put out, the better it'll be for you and your business. In this chapter I'm going to show you a strategy that will help you maximize your content output. It's possible to create months' worth of content in just a few days. Yes, that means you'll have to put in some hard work for a little while, but it'll pay off soon enough. This is the same strategy that Peng Joon used to launch his career and to continue to dominate the content marketing game. If you have no idea who he is, look him up because he's generating a good living by the work he does.

I'm mostly going to be talking about breaking down video content, but you can utilize this strategy with blogs, podcasts, and any other forms of content that you'd like to create as well. This formula is going to help you broadcast your message on multiple different platforms at once, so if you've done your homework and learned about a couple of the platforms we talked about, then this is going to help you dominate those platforms.

If you happen to be reading this, and some of those platforms no longer exist, you can still utilize this strategy to be more productive and free up your time to do other things for your business. So let's jump into making things happen!

Phase 1: Shoot 120 videos in 3 days – 3-5 minutes in length.

We've discussed strategies on how to shoot good videos in chapter 3 so if you need a refresher, go back and check those out. You know best what your channel or profile is focused on, so these videos need to have a clear message that relates to the vision of your channel and what you'd like to accomplish. Do some research on Buzzsumo, Answerthepublic or Quora and see what people are searching for in your niche.

After that craft headlines that'll catch people's attention and help you create videos on specific topics. Here is a list of phrases that performed the best on

Facebook in 2017:

1. will make you

2. this is why

3. can we guess

4. only x in (x = a number)

5. the reason is

6. are freaking out

7. x stunning photos

8. tears of joy

9. is what happens

10. make you cry

11. give you goosebumps

12. talking about it

13. is too cute

14. shocked to see

15. melt your heart

16. x things only

17. can't stop laughing

18. top x songs

19. Twitter reacts to

20. what happened next

See if you can incorporate any of these headlines or something similar to craft your own and plan out your video ideas. Do your best to make them informative, valuable, and entertaining. You don't have to have all three in every video for them to be good, but at least quality in each will be beneficial for you.

Title each of your videos something clear, and easy for you to find. By titling your videos what you'll be titling them on social media, you'll be setting your content up to be found with SEO before you even upload it anywhere.

Phase 2: Repurpose your video into text

We talked about repurposing your content a little bit in chapter 2, it means taking one piece of content and using it again in a different format. Here you'll take those 120 videos that you shot and bring them into either rev.com or designrr.io, I prefer designrr because you can pay a monthly fee to get a good amount of video converted, whereas with Rev you have to pay for each video individually. Go to https://go.brimagraphics.com/designrr to get started now.

Phase 3: Edit videos for the various platforms

We've discussed how videos formatted one way will work on YouTube, but may not work on Facebook. So keep in mind different formats, Instagram use 864x1080, Facebook either 1080x720 or 864x1080, YouTube 1920x1080 or 1080x720. Add subtitles to each video, and if you want to stand out, create a frame to go around your videos for Instagram and Facebook.

Phase 4 – Uploading and scheduling your content

Upload your videos to the platforms you want them to be on, and schedule them to be released on certain days. If you have 120 videos, you can put one out every day for about four months. Facebook and YouTube allow you to schedule posts in advance, and you can also use sites like Buffer.com to schedule them on platforms that don't let you do that. For sites like YouTube it's advantageous to fill in the keywords section with keywords used by the top ranking videos similar to yours. And don't forget to fill in the about section with what your video is about and your links for people to find your products and services. You'll also need eye-catching thumbnails to stand out in a busy crowd.

Phase 5 – Create other types of posts

Now that you've transcribed all of your videos and uploaded them, you can also create different types of posts. The entire transcripts can be used for blog posts, and long posts on Facebook, and Instagram. Just find pictures you can use with each post to catch people's attention.

You can also take short quotes from the transcriptions and put them over your images. Quote, type pictures do really well on social media because people resonate with their message right away. They're short and punchy, and can easily get good engagement which will only be to your advantage.

The videos can also easily be converted into audio format and used as podcast episodes. This is the format I do for Brimo Live Journey To 6 Figures. I shoot a Facebook live and then upload the audio to anchor.fm. Another idea is taking the audio files and putting a short clip over a picture to make a video. The possibilities are endless and I hope you have a lot of fun experimenting with different types of posts. You'll easily be able to post multiple times a day which all of the social media platforms like.

If you utilize this content strategy, you'll have content for at least four months. That's more than most people ever post on social media. So if you want to get ahead this is the way to go. It takes a lot of time at first, but after you schedule everything you get to sit back and watch the magic play out in front of your eyes.

By posting frequently on the platforms, their algorithms will allow your content to get in front of more people. If you want to expedite the process you can boost your posts or create paid ads. I highly recommend this strategy, but you need a budget for it to be successful.

Chapter 12 Putting It All Together

Think about all of the content that has caught your attention over the years. Whether it's been TV commercials, viral videos, or just posts you resonated with. What made them catch your eye? One of my favorite videos of all time is the "Myspace Movie." In high school when Myspace was still fairly new David Lehre created a spoof called the "Myspace Movie" and in my opinion it was HILARIOUS! It made fun of all the things we loved to hate about Myspace and how crazy social media was when it was first coming out. Things like taking obnoxious selfies in the bathroom, being catfished, top friends and even chain letters.

It's done over a million views on YouTube and I even went back to watch it as I was typing this part of the book out. I wanted to be reminded about why I loved it in the first place and the biggest reason is that it was so relatable at the time. My friends and I watched it so many times and shared it dozens more. I was even inspired to create my own Myspace movie that ended up winning an award at a fine arts competition.

The content we like impacts us and when we like it we like, share it, comment, and even watch it over and over again. I hope this book has inspired you to start creating content that other people can't help but be inspired to take action with! Whether they engage with it, share it, or even purchase your products/services because of it.

My goal is for you to have a better understanding of not only how social media works, but also how you can use it to your advantage to further your business or your brand. We've gone over some of the different social media platforms, what types of content there are, how to come up with endless content ideas, how to make your content stand out on social media, how to connect with your audience and start to solve their problems so you can get paid.

This book is a great reference for putting all of the pieces together as you go about your social media presence and grow your following. Don't be afraid to post! Taking action is what will propel your progress forward, not waiting for things to happen. You'll be waiting a long time, then all of the social media algorithms will change and you'll be stuck in the same spot. With no one knowing who you are, and not making any money. So if you want to be seen as an authority figure, if you want people to know who you are, if you want your message to be heard, and if you want to help as many people as possible, then start implementing now!

Social media is an incredible tool for us today and when you leverage it you'll see some amazing results! The book may end here, but that doesn't mean our relationship has to. I want to continue the conversation and further your education by creating amazing content. That's why I've created the Social 7 Content Creation Course. This course is going to help you do everything we've gone over in this book with real-life examples you can see and study for yourself. It's also going to cover everything I couldn't have put into just one little book like this.

So if you're ready to learn more and grow as a content creator then head over to www.s7challenge.com/order-page. You can sign up for my content creation course and also snag a ton of bonuses that'll help you with your content creation and growing your business.

I enjoyed being able to put together a handbook like this so that more people could start using social media to bring awareness to their brand, message, and incredible products and services because I know the amazing impact they can have! You were put here on this planet to make an impact and an incredible difference. I hope I can somehow help you on your quest. Feel free to reach out to me on social media. You can find me @brimomorales on Facebook and Instagram, and @brimothecoolest on Twitter. The next section of the book has my closing thoughts and some resources for you to continue your content creation journey. These are tools that I've used to grow my business and I know they can work for you too.

Good luck with all that you are pursuing. I believe in you.

Now You've Got to Believe

Thank you so much for reading my book! I am so grateful that you picked it up, paid for it and had the wherewithal to finish it. Not everyone that picks up a book will finish it, but because you did I wanted to give you a little bit of extra wisdom before we part ways.

Now forgive me if I start to sound a little woo-woo, or out there, but I do believe that we are all extremely powerful human beings once we tap into our true selves. A lot of us go on thinking that we can't accomplish things, but in reality that's not true. If it were, no one would ever be successful and we already know many people are out there crushing it! So the main thing you've got to hold onto is the belief that you can be successful.

There will come days when it's harder to post content on your social media, email your list, or learn something new. There will be days when all you want to do is curl up in bed or beat your head against the wall. When those days come around hold onto why you're on this journey in the first place. Why do you need to be successful? Who's counting on you to pull it off? Do it for them! Do it for yourself! But most importantly, hold onto the belief that all of this is possible and that you'll achieve success!

You can make 6 or 7 figures with social media, you can create the business of your dreams, it's possible to take your company from 1 million to 10 million! Anything is possible but you've got to believe it first. I'm a huge proponent of the law of attraction. If you're not familiar with the law of attraction, it says that if you focus on all of the negative aspects of your life, then all you'll attract are more negative moments in your life; but instead, if you focus on all of the positive things in your life, you'll attract more positive things.

I've tested out this theory myself, and I can tell you that when I focus on all of the wonderful things in my life and am truly grateful for all of them, I find myself attracting more things to be grateful for! I've been able to attract my wife, money for a trip, gift cards, and all sorts of other great things in my life. For instance, back in 2018 I wanted to attend a week-long self-development workshop. The only problem was I didn't have enough money to cover the costs. So I sat and visualized myself there. I saw myself with my friends that were going and imagined us having a great time. During the weeks leading up to the event, I allowed myself to be open to the idea that the money for the event would come. I didn't know how and I didn't know when, but I believed that the money would come.

A few weeks before the event was set to take place, I posted on social media asking for ideas to come up with the money. I got lots of ideas but, I also got something I never expected. One of my marketing friends messaged me and said, "I believe in you, if you can come up with half of the money you need for the trip, I'll cover the other half." This completely blew my mind! I wasn't expecting this from anyone and I didn't ask anyone for money, he just wanted to give it to me. So I thanked him tremendously and kept brainstorming ideas.

Not long after the first friend messaged me, another friend told me they were giving me their deposit to go to the same event because their plans had changed. Then, someone else gave me a little bit more and before I knew it, I had exactly the amount of money I needed to get there! Within 3 days I went from not knowing how I was going to get to the event, to having flights booked and everything else set! That event was extremely beneficial to me and my work! I am forever grateful that everything came together for me to experience everything I did there. And I'm not the only person that's been able to do this, so have a lot of other people in the world.

You can be one of those people too! All you have to do is believe, stay focused on your goal, and appreciate all of the progress you make along the way. I wanted to make sure I set you up with the best chance to win so I couldn't leave out this last little secret to help guide you on your journey. This is only the tip of the law of attraction iceberg, so if you want to learn more about it there will be books in the resources section that you can check out later on.

This book is also a manifestation of mine. I wanted to become a published author someday, but I didn't know how I was going to be able to do that. Now I know, when you're ready, everything lines up in your favor and things start happening! Now that this book is here, I'm hoping to help multitudes learn how to use these tools to grow their businesses, create income for their families, and make a big difference in this world.

A portion of the proceeds from the sale of this book is going to help me start a senior dog rescue here in my hometown of San Antonio, Texas. To see progress, feel free to follow me on social media, I've got my links in the resources section. That's the next vision I've got and this book is just one step of getting me to that dream fulfilled. So thank you so much again for purchasing my book and helping me to save senior dogs' lives! I hope this has helped you in some way. If it has, please leave me a five-star review on Amazon so we can get this out to help more people on their online marketing journey.

Resources

Now that you've finished this book you should be proud of yourself! You took the time to learn how to take your social media game to the next level. I also wanted this book to be a guide that you can come back to time and time again when you need new ideas or when you want some more tools to help you with your content journey. So here I'm going to give you a list of tools to help you with your business.

1. Clickfunnels-This is a great funnel building software that will work for any business. You can grab a two-week free trial by going to https://go.brimagraphics.com/clickfunnels

2. Bluehost- This is a site that will host your domain and make it easier to build a wordpress site, it's also super affordable and you can get a discount by going to https://go.brimagraphics.com/bluehost

3. Namecheap – This site is useful for buying domains cheaply and also for

hosting services. I really like this platform. www.namecheap.com

4. Designrr – This website is good for repurposing your content, you can get a membership by

going here https://go.brimagraphics.com/designrr

5. The Social 7 Challenge – Want to be guided in a week long content creation challenge? I've

put that together inside of The Social 7 Challenge and I'd love for you to take part in the next

one. Every day for seven days you'll receive a prompt to write a post about on your social media

profile that will help you start getting engagement right away. There's even daily trainings for

each day. It's completely free and you can register by going to www.s7challenge.com

6. Content Creation Course – If you want to skip the challenge and go right into learning how to

create amazing content, then jump into The Social 7 Content Creation Course! Inside there's

hours of video lessons that will help you on your content journey and maximize your ability to build your audience, earn their trust, and start converting. You can snag that by going to https://www.s7challenge.com/order-page

7. Online Marketing Genius Facebook Group – Inside this community of other online marketers you can continue the conversation after this book. If you have any questions or want insight into your marketing you can find it here. I even do live trainings once a week to go over more marketing techniques. You can even request a marketing review. To join this group and to become an online marketing genius then go to here

https://go.brimagraphics.com/OMGGroup

8. Get Response – Once you get people in your funnel you're going to need to email them to build relationships with your audience. Get Response is a super easy to use website that helps you email vast amounts of people at once. You can grab a free trial by going to https://go.brimagraphics.com/getresponse

9. Fiverr – This is a great website to start outsourcing things to. Let's say you need someone to video edit for you, or create a book cover, even design a

logo for you, it can all be done here and more at a relatively low cost. www.fiverr.com

10. Funnel Rolodex – This is another great website for outsourcing and the people here are very familiar with funnels and what you need to have in them. So if you're wanting to launch your first funnel but don't want to build it, then head over here. www.funnelrolodex.com

11. Anchor – This is a great site to publish a podcast to for free! You'll be on some of the most popular podcast platforms all at once. It's super easy to get started and I highly recommend using it. www.anchor.fm

12. Buffer – This site helps you to schedule out your content on up to three social media platforms for free! It's super easy to use and I love it! You can get a paid version for more profiles if you wish, but this is definitely a good one. www.buffer.com

13. IFTTT – I like this website because what it does is link a bunch of your social media accounts so when you post something on Instagram it'll post directly on Twitter, or maybe you upload a YouTube video and it goes to Facebook. It's really convenient! www.ifttt.com

14. Buzzsumo – This site is perfect for staying up to date with what's trending in the world. You definitely want to stay relevant and this site can help you do just that! www.buzzsumo.com

Books

1. The Secret by Rhonda Byrne – This is a basic introduction to the Law of Attraction. There's also a movie by the same name which has a lot of the same info as the book. If you're new to the idea of the Law of Attraction I highly recommend starting here.

2. The Power of Intention by Dr. Wayne Dyer – I absolutely love this book! It goes over the idea of setting your intention to how you want your life to be and goes into detail on how to attract those things into your life.

3. <u>Wishes Fulfilled by Dr. Wayne Dyer</u> – This is a perfect companion to The Power of Intention and will also help you in the manifesting department. I loved this book as well!

4. <u>Ask And It Is Given by Abraham Hicks</u> – This is another good introduction into the Law of Attraction and creating the life you desire.

5. <u>Jab Jab Jab, Right Hook By Gary Vaynerchuk</u> – This book is really great because it talks about how to use the best types of posts for the different social media platforms. So if you're wanting some more insight then grab it!

6. <u>Crushing It! By Gary Vaynerchuk</u> – This book is proof that if you want to make something happen with social media, it's possible! Now is the time to jump in and kill it. Gary Vee gives you examples of people that used his advice from his first book Crush It and are super successful now, you should definitely check it out.

7. Dotcom Secrets by Russel Brunson – This book is perfect if you're new to building funnels and all things online marketing. There's scripts to use when talking to your clients and even more tips on how to put all the pieces together. You can grab a free copy at https://go.brimagraphics.com/dotcom-secrets

8. Expert Secrets by Russel Brunson – This book is a great next steps book after you've read Dotcom Secrets and have been marketing for a little while, because it talks about creating a completely new offer from scratch. It really shows you how to create a movement and make traction to build your following and get your sales going with a converting webinar. I highly recommend this book if you want to sell high ticket products and services. Grab your free copy by going to https://go.brimagraphics.com/expert-secrets

9. Unconscious Branding by Douglas Van Praet – This book is incredible when it comes to marketing and what makes people want to buy your product. I literally could not put this book down because it had so much good information in it! I recommend it to everyone!

10. You Are a Badass at Making Money by Jen Sincero – This is one of my all-time favorite books and I tell everyone to read it! This is the first book that put a fire under my butt and made me believe that I could actually get all of this stuff to work for me. If you're struggling with mindset and believing in yourself, this book can help you become a money magnet!

11. The Attractor Factor by Dr. Joe Vitale – I recently read through this one again and I'm so glad I did! This book is amazing when it comes to getting everything you want. The author Dr. Vitale, marries spirituality with business in an incredible way and if you're at all spiritual I recommend you grab this book and study it over and over.

12. Traffic Secrets by Russel Brunson – This is the newest book from Russel Brunson and it's absolutely incredible! Now that you know how to use social media to get people to your offer, this book helps you get even more eyeballs on your stuff! I highly recommend grabbing your copy by going to https://go.brimagraphics.com/trafficsecrets

The conversation doesn't have to end here!

Connect with me:

www.instagram.com/brimomorales

www.facebook.com/brimomorales

www.brimomorales.com

@brimothecoolest on Twitter

brimo@brimagraphics.com

www.ingramcontent.com/pod-product-compliance
Lightning Source LLC
Chambersburg PA
CBHW071414210526
45465CB00001B/387